Number 1

UNCERTAIN THE FINAL RUN TO WINTER

UNCERTAIN THE FINAL RUN TO WINTER

by

William Kloefkorn

Many of the poems in this book originally appeared in the following magazines: *Apple, Crazy Horse, December, Hanging Loose, Hiram Poetry Review, Kansas Quarterly, Karamu, Midwest Quarterly, Monmouth Review, Mustang Review, Ohio University Review, Omaha World-Herald, Pebble, Poem, Poet & Critic, The New Salt Creek Reader, Saltillo, South Florida Poetry Journal*, and *Wisconsin Review*.

"Uncertain the Final Run to Winter" was first printed in *Prairie Schooner*, Copyright © 1971 by the University of Nebraska Press.

ISBN 0-931534-07-0

Additional copies of this book may be ordered by mail from Windflower Press, 1720½ C. Street, Lincoln, Nebraska 68502.

Third Printing

UNCERTAIN THE FINAL RUN TO WINTER

Summer,
a fat horse
tender against the spurs.

Now as the last edge of autumn
hangs precipiced in yellow on the trees
the animal sees the sudden space and shies.
I sense the ropy girth go loose:
uncertain the final run to winter.

Between the halt and the beginning
lies the gap,
familiar to the eye
as palm to pommel.

My lean horse balks: ahead,
the wide white skylessness of space.

Not knowing where mount and rider end,
or where they come together,
I see myself as statue weathered,
sitting its saddle like an Ichabod.

COUNTRY BOY

Today a south wind rises,
bearing boyhood's grim effluvium.
(Once I was invited to a posh estate
reigned over by him whose head
has since been bronzed, and there
I reached for the wrong fork.)
It is that sort of day:
the warm wind, up from Kansas,
has bad breath.
(And I remember the night
I failed to wet the bed,
but at the height of pride
discovered urine, stout as cateyes,
in a dresser drawer.)
It is that sort of August day,
precisely:
bedsheets snapping on the line,
the scent of oxblood, tart as ensilage,
rising from the spitshine
on these Saturday night shoes.

FAIRPORT

According to Stocker,
most of the people
that do their serious shopping here
are too muleheaded ever to pass on.
That's why sometimes at night
you can hear a rattling from the graveyard:
Republicans and Democrats, Methodists and Baptists,
all at each others' empty throats.
In the oval frames
that decorate the bank
are faces of the first fathers,
and when an old man dies
his son, or someone's,
rises full-blown from the ceremonial dust.
Bones and eyebrows everywhere,
according to Stocker,
some of them still alive and lifted,
wearing out the storefronts
on a Saturday night.
They stretch as far south
as the mind can see,
Stocker says,
then two days west:
from Maine to Medicine Lodge,
from time to Timbuktu,
from hell to breakfast.

ZELMA LEE CRENSHAW

At our first homemade peepshow
Zelma Lee Crenshaw was the only one
to go all the way,
lifting her second and final leg
from her white panties,
which before she pivoted slowly to face us
she tossed back over her right shoulder--
whereupon that simple space of silk,
as luck would have it,
slid like a shrine on bearings
precisely to where I sat crosslegged
on Zelma Lee's mother's hard fastidious floor.
Then did Zelma Lee, as if long at practice,
turn inch by inch to show herself,
her small, flawless, oval face,
her bosoms like grapes,
the joining of her legs
a creampuff neatly creased.
Only in her eyes,
which were green
and quite large for their age,
was Zelma Lee Crenshaw,
who by now was laughing,
crying.

CLEANING OUT MY DEAD GRANDFATHER'S BARN

A sudden flash of light
No larger than a dime
Told me that human hands
Had worn the pommel to newness
Where old leather had been.

But today the human hands
Went dead a final time.
Piling harness and saddle away,
Cantle and stirrup, singletree,
Checkrein, blinder and hame,

I saw the sudden flash
Of Granddad in the coin
Of light: his hands without
Splotches lay like the power
Of horseflesh tugging to join

Gray seasons to this fresh September.
Then heartlessly the hands
Went dull: no more. Just the
Heavy hide of cracked
Harness, a broken bellyband,

And cruppers rubbed with the brown
Of fifty years of dung.
I piled it all in the pickup
And drove it quickly away
From the low-angled autumn sun.

OTOE COUNTY IN NEBRASKA

On the run is the Otoe County corn rootworm,
overcome by laboratories:
who have purpled the soil with nuggets enough
to deter the deepest scavenger.
Thus as you drive the plush curvaceous trails
of Otoe County
you can sense the rootworm's grim retreat--
the dirty little no good
crop killing bugger
hightailing it for Kansas and Oklahoma,
for south Texas,
through Mexico
to a tip in Yucatan
from which it can throw itself
for mercy into the sea.
You can imagine it going without breakfast,
halfway now across the Caribbean,
dogpaddling its hundred thousand legs
to maintain a slim distance
between its life's little juice
and the laboratories that,
running at full throttle with periscope up,
cannot unlock their hatches until that
last little juice has been spilled.

Meanwhile, back in Otoe County,
the cornrows rise corpulent as green trees.
In a red Volkswagen you are a snail,
hunched and alien and terribly humble.

DEC. 8, 1941

Sound travels to tell us
Not of something ended
But of something begun.
So in the early morning,

During the hour for arithmetic,
Jackie Dellman stands alone,
Privileged in the cloakroom,
Crying without raising his hands

Before a clear bright pane
Of window. Yesterday the Japanese
Bombed his big brother at
Pearl Harbor; today the sound of the

Rising Sun is rich with bravado
And fear and the slight vibrant
Embarrassment of seated schoolboys
Calculating their new classmate,

Who only two days ago celebrated Friday
By bloodying the taller nose
Of a red-haired confident
Fifth grader, but who now,

On this peculiar Monday morning,
Weeps at the window with the
Cloakroom door open, weeps
With his victorious fists

Dangling like bandages at his sides,
His bare grief confounding all
Human equations. Yet I with others
Hear and work with it; it

Enters my wooden desk
To travel up my spine
To finally force a whiteness
Upon the foreign fingers that

Clutch at pencils. There seems
To be no stopping it,
It that rose how long
Before the rising of the

Rising sun, that slid inviolable
Over calm international airways
At how many hundred feet-per-second
To tell the Emperor that he owns

The world and must dispose of
Jackie Dellman's brother,
To become the whistle of bomb-fins
On a soundless Sunday morning,

To be the keen of boyhood
And the wail of silent
Bewildered mathematicians,
Their long division growing forever

Longer: who in this conflagration
First spoke of fire? And who
Will be the last to shout its heat
Into the cool quotient of emptiness?

PRIME MOVING

I think of scrap lumber
Going warped behind our toilet,
And of Father, bent like bad pine,
Putting a pipe wrench to plumbing strange as neckties.

Of unlikely pieces that make all linkage possible:
Of the toilet, August dry--
Like Kansas creeks puffed white with sand,
Parching, twisting, waiting for water;
Of the lumber, scrapped but handy,
Askew like fiddlesticks;
Of the match I threw that day,
Its tipend hot as the high sun;
Of the rabbit that startled bounced away
From the accidental flame,
And of Mother, big eyed,
Blowing into her apron a nose
Bereft of its family convenience.

Until by evening, when the smoke
Had cleared and Mother felt God's hot hand
Gentle upon her brow. It all means indoor plumbing,
She said, and *now*.

Even today I hear the words
And think of matches,
Of the fleeing rabbit,
Of scrap lumber and the tiny tilted shed,
Of Father, bent like bad pine,
Putting a pipe wrench to plumbing strange as neckties.

And of the new porcelain bowl
So beautiful
It might have been Christ feeding the multitude.

THE REARRANGING

Stocker used to say that something
is seldom reduced to nothing
by the wind. Chiefly, he said,
it's a matter of rearranging.
That's why sometimes you see a leghorn
shivering down Main Street,
naked as a needle,
or a phone pole growing feathers.
What the wind picked up an hour ago
it'll deposit tomorrow,
according to Stocker,
and sooner or later it picks up
damn near everything:
bedsheets and shingles
and hubcaps and small children
and the spoken word, even,
and the remotest odor.
Stocker claimed that on a clear night,
when the wind goes suddenly calm,
you can hear the pyramids being built,
can catch with the flaring of a nostril
the brief, sweet stench of kings.

ROSASHARN

Hundreds of early souls have been interred
deep in the sunscorched shale
northeast of Sharon.
There, a red rock
like a gross unlikely flower
blooms, porous and incongruous
among the bunch grass.
It must have been an obese pioneer
that straggling on a hot day
waved schooner and kinfolk on,
then settled once and for all
its grim ungainly bones.

Nor does it budge when truants down from Spivey
scrape something of their lives
into its osseous skin.
There, hardened Catholics
break bread with the damned.
There only is Melba Jean available,
does Russell B. love Gloria.
Approach it on a warm June day,
when the sky is high
and the cattle, curious,
seem impossible to spook.
Read it as you would
a tree, a bridge, a barn.
Call it, for want of a lustier name,
the Rose of Sharon.

LTL

Carry A. Nation came into our house and filled it
With her meagerness. She was hung full-fleshed
Against the flowered wallpaper of our living-room,
And Mrs. Wilma Hunt, who brought her, gave each
Of us a little wooden hatchet. "John Barleycorn
Is the Devil," Mrs. Wilma Hunt said. And
By dropping worms head-
First into alcohol she taught us
To hate him. "Now let me tell
You," she said, "about the LTL..."

She taught us the Loyal
Temperance Legion song, all of it, then killed
Another worm and served refreshments. Our house
Had never been so full. There were all of us, with
Carry on the wall-
Paper: Kool-Aid, Cookies, Song,
Something-New-to-Hate--
And several dead worms
Curled in alcohol.

TOWN TEAM

The local jocks back home in Attica
seem more than amply snugged.

At first base a stomach extends itself
to scoop a low throw, like a gunslug,
from the dust.

The shortstop moves like a sweet fat fairy
to his right or left,
his sneakers leaking ballbearings.

Outfielders jog for several days to their positions,
pivot like bloated ballerinas,
doff their caps,
then jog for several days back to the dugout.

The infield is a squat and pussel-gutted chain.
Round faced and red, it
chews its tongue and
spits practically perfect daisies.

The pitcher trembles the mound with a headshake:
he wants another sign.
The catcher, wide as a sandcrab,
sweats marbles.

At the plate
a batter settles into his stance
like a tender, untapped keg.

SOME DIRECTIONS FOR THE DECEMBER
TOURING OF WESTCENTRAL NEBRASKA

Turn right at the Standard Station
And head due west. Do not
Eat at the Hungry Indian
In Ogallala or stop for

Free tea at the Big Farmer
In Oshkosh--By Gosh. My
Advice, Sir: go cold and
Hungry over these wintered ranges

Where only on a cloudless night
Can the sky outstrip the land.
Join the tumbleweed. Huddle
With herefords against leeward

Walls. Walk barefoot over
Steaming dung along the
Dormant seeded rows of
Next year's yield. Forget

The motels at North Platte,
Tune out all noisy Teepees:
KODY, KOLT, KCOW. Hum
The notes of rusting cultivators

And watch with the hawk
For mice and rabbits and
Scott's once-in-a-lifetime bluff.
Inhale. Go dizzy with the

Windmill. Stretch even the
Fingertips against sand-coated hills.
You can get there from here,
Sir. But you must go

Cold and hungry. That route is best.
Just forget your Pontiac, then
Turn right at the Standard Station
And drive due west.

THE SPRING HOUSE

Seeping upward from some deep sense
Of purity, our spring gathers
Itself like the shaping of a birth
Inside the damp hush of unweathered

Stone. It rises to fill the basin
That Grandfather poured, to flow unrippling
Down a concrete trough toward sunlight
And a vast world's deeper swifter stream.

The square brown stones that shape the house
Speak our respect. Under rockless skies
They shelter what we have to need:
The pressing of an open eye

Onto clarity. I kneel beyond
All kneeling to see what seems to be
The source, its shade the gravelled sand
Scouring my impure memory.

Inside the soundless house I touch
The water with dry lips, drinking
The cool life of an unborn catfish
That in our pasture on a winding

Muddied stream sleeps belly-buried
At the bottom of a hole. The coolness
Is like a sudden flushed repose
That drives even sweat before its rest.

There is no wind in the spring house,
No weather; the air is water rising.
With it I rise, fulfilled. The sun
Is a network of screen-door, glaring

Upon all deeper swifter streams.
But it cannot change the stone spring house:
Memory stands inviolate in
The shaded place where all times pass.

I leave the spring house only to
Return, to breathe barefooted
Upon the clarity that joins
The muddy miracle of uprooted

Universes. For it is the source
Of Afton that I seek and dread,
Compelled to marvel at movement and
To worship visible fountainheads.

FLOYD FENTON

Mandrake the Magician,
who is sometimes Floyd Fenton,
engages the pinball machine,
bets a beer that he has
quicker wrists.
Which he has,
so much so that by midnight
his kidneys could float a cruiser.
Over the rims of dying cans
the competition drools,
the great magician meanwhile
growing ever larger--
until by dawn he is so bloated
he can scarcely lift a leg:
thus with help on every side,
Mandrake the Magician is handled
out of the pool hall
and into the cab
of his pickup.
There, he sleeps
the sleep of the dead,
his pink face rooted
deep as a kiss
into the wide mute mouth
of the steering wheel.

ELSIE MARTIN

She's six of one, half a dozen of another,
According to Stocker:
Not a bad looker, for a widowwoman,
But her face so knobbed with indecision
You'd swear she has hemorrhoids.
Heard of another case just like her,
He said,
Who starved to death in a grocery store,
Comparing labels.
Always and forever between a rock and a hard place--
Not fishing, quite,
And not quite cutting bait.
So precisely between the devil
And the deep blue sea
That she lives with one foot in heaven
And the other in hot water.
Split her right down the middle,
Stocker said,
And it wouldn't make a dime's worth of difference
Which half you reached for.

PREACHER

for Louis DeGrazia

Smell the preacher.
He is a Butler County Baptist,
come wet from hell with
the glory and the wonder and the horror
of the Lord.
He has gone from Eden to Armageddon
to Thelma's Diner, all in a single evening,
and now, wide and alone in the corner booth,
he seems no more chosen
than the unattended jawbone
of an ass.
He has ordered chicken-fried steak,
heavy on sauce and onion,
so that his private aura eventually
is joined to the juices
of a public paradise:
sweat, salt, saliva, hashbrowns, bay rum,
cream-and-sugared coffee lolled on the tongue
like a safe temptation.
The preacher
chews with his mouth open,
has nothing to hide.
His thumbnails bear the honest grit
of a temporal life.
His teeth, amid the oxblood sauce,
show sharp and white.
His face is flushed,
his blue eyes round and luminous and moist,
his hair a copy of a slick young Solomon.
Later, the diner door eased shut behind him,
he will break wind gently,
will fit himself then to the contours
of his Studebaker
and with a grunt of gears
peel up and out and away,
leaving a smattering of elect
to ponder a benediction
rife with rubber and
unfettered fumes.

THE BULL IN SIMPSON'S PASTURE

The bull in Simpson's pasture,
like an addict,
returns to the ledge,
stands there muted in his hot heavy pride.
his nostrils flared in absolute disbelief
at the sudden immense hole
that like a mad magician's joke
yawns down and out before him.

The bull is king of Simpson's pasture,
yet he has never yet walked one step further
than the lordship of his deepest sense allows.
Almost daily he ambles from the herd,
his hard hooves tempted to the brink.
Behind him, and beyond the opening,
the lambent prairie undulates,
pocked only by the woodchuck and the mole.

The bull, both jealous and afraid,
paws gently at the emptiness,
seems to begrudge his kingdom
this its only incongruity.
Without warning, beyond all reason, it occurs,
and the bull, on schedule at its edge,
cannot forgive that which tolerates
not even one transgression.

Yet the bull will choose once more to view it,
will leave the grazing to his lovely cows
to try again:
and will again relent,
will back away again,
that first step like the ripping out of ligaments.
And, between the haunches,
an ache more royal than stone.

RUBY

One of Christ's unwanted many,
Ruby rotted right along with the porch swing.
It started in the mind, they say,
And ended chiefly in the teeth and dugs.
How she knew the good Lord never gave her anything:
Not even, mind you, a decent pot to pee in.
Thus the grim corrosiveness of urine,
Working at the edges of the brain, the husband.
Then to the dog, the children.
And, at last, the porch swing.
On which alas sat Ruby--
Not a grinder in her head, her breasts unclean--
Rocking her pure despair,
Like a stillborn child,
Into the vast satanic hush of evenings.

OUTSTATE NEBRASKA, NOV. 21

The boys at the power plant are talking snow.

Outside of Thelma's Popper
the smell of buttered corn
balances on near icy air like some
firm unpainted farm girl
riding bareback.

In the pool hall hovered under smoke
are quartets singing dominoes.

Beer lies in oak lakes at the bar.

Outside, Floyd Catlett sits a bench
that fifty years ago
might have been a mare.
He lips a fresh cigarette,
feeling his mackinaw for matches.

The custodian at the United Methodist Church
is wondering where to go
to ask a question or two
about thermostats.

The cook at Bake's Cafe expects a light supper run.

Judy Garland is at the Rialto.
Yellow bulbs blink on the marquee,
while low lamps light asphalt
up and down the street.

Breath goes neat as Sunday shirts.

From somewhere gloves clap.
Beyond the sound, darkness.
The heavy smell of clouds.

Snow, sure as hell!

Beside dynamos
the boys at the power plant
smile and spit stoutly
through their brown teeth.

RENDEZVOUS

Bonnie?
I'll meet you tonight near the pond.
Sundown.
Second log from the left.
You bring the shovel, I'll bring the gills.
We can tunnel our way, as usual,
To the water, then drift with the turtles.
And forget the full moon,
Dear Bonnie,
And the goose you say
Is roosting on your grave:
There is little chance of our being uncovered,
Of our ever not being saved.
We will return again upright
In unobtrusive skin,
Our fingers parted and
All moss brushed cleanly from the gums
We fit our white appearances in.

Bonnie?
I'll see you this evening, then.
And stop worrying about the meeting:
Neither of my wives, and
None of our living spawn,
Suspects a thing.

W. P. HANSON

Halfway through its
diagnosis of a carburetor
W. P. Hanson's left eye
recalls the unfinished mending
of Harvey Klinglesmith's spare tire,
whose tube with its new coldpatch
has been pressing in the vice overnight
until now as W. P. Hanson releases it
it looks like a red eye
in the center of a black waffle,
which W. P. Hanson stuffs
between the rim and the tire
until, hearing a voice at the door,
he drops both hands at the same time
and moments later is up to his elbows
in spare greasy parts,
dead certain that the proof
from the 63 Plymouth is there somewhere,
the car itself not far away either,
precisely where it was retreated from
only yesterday morning when W. P. Hanson
left an unboxed U-joint in the oilpit
to rip loose a rusted muffler
that he hopes to have the right mounts for
by the time he finishes
with Lloyd Turner's Chevy.

W. P. Hanson's wife meanwhile
lies on her bed in her bedroom,
naked on her back,
her inside thighs dry as new zerks.
Her eyes are wide open,
and she is saying
Bill? Bill? Bill?

THE CHINKING

Detectives swarming the acreage:
Yet far below the level of the storm
Our basement, seeping.
Squirrels and starlings in the attic,
Nursing, grinning.
I have told the Dicks
To shoot on sight to kill:
Yet the pond below is
Deepening, spreading.
Even now the systematic rain
Is broken by a dripping:
O Mama dear,
Our rooftop, leaking!
What can we do with such a place
Now that at last it's ours,
But leaning?
The ragbag is empty,
And our final underwear cannot alone
Provide the chinking.
Surely that much we know,
O Mama dear,
And in the bones.
Why is it then we linger here,
Bare skinned among the moss and frogs,
Settling, planning?

MARVEL RODERICK

Took her green thumb with her everywhere,
into the greenhouse that used to be her garage
(until a tornado,
providentially in cahoots
with Marvel Roderick's thumb,
decided otherwise),
where planters by the score
could not contain their multifoliate buds,
along the blacktop into town,
where at the motion of her wondrous thumb
week-long vegetables in Vernon Potter's unswept store
began again to bloom:
and rumor had it
that once she touched a wren's egg into life,
touched then the wet wings dry
and with a single motion of her thumb
presumed the bird to fly.

Some folks are simply gifted that way,
according to Stocker:
so it was actually no single mortal's fault
that Stella Cleveland's husband,
for example,
couldn't control himself--
and that all over Marvel's farm,
in chinks and cracks and unattended doors,
children sprung up full-blown, almost,
almost like flowers.

RUSSELL CALVERT

Russell owned a green Ford coupe
and went out of his way
to run over animals,
especially cats—
which I used to think
endeared him to Peggy McKaig,
who was always on his right arm
like a very well-developed appendage.
But I was wrong.
Peggy told me herself
she stayed with Russ that long
only to try and change himl
That when she saw
how hopeless his case was,
how the edge of his right eye
warmed only at the instant of impact,
she switched over to me.

WALKING DOWN MAIN STREET ON A SATURDAY NIGHT, WEARING CLEAN OVERALLS AND A NEW HAIRCUT

Singing of Sweet-Pea Talcum
And of Bay Rum
I am for one fine flash
Cocksure of my salvation:

O Jesus loves me,
That I know,
For my fragrance tells me so!

I am sweetness,
I am light,
I am the bush
That burns a blue deliverance
Through the night.

To me, as to an altar,
Even the hopeless come,
Sniffing the Alpha of creation.

Like children
They touch my garment's hem,
And like a gentle Jove I move
In gentleness about them.

Amid an aura rich with myrrh
I sanforize the earth,
And call it good.

O I am the blood washed resurrection
Bearing its nectar to a soulless Sodom!

I am the one Zacchaeus climbed to see,
The usurers abhorred:
The one to whom the Judas
Of my awed assembly cried,
"Hey, Willie,
I see you finally got your fat ears lowered!"

TOOTS SLOCUM

Black magic yet in the words Toots Slocum,
who like all natural incomparables
came into this world
with the same basic apparatus
she circumcised our backfield with.
How else explain the opening loss to Kiowa?
And the way we ran at Medicine Lodge!
Goons, goons, goons,
gooneyes aglint like little silver marbles,
goonhands bearing the pigskin
like a brown leather chalice
directly to the sideline,
to the airborne X where Toots Slocum
sprawled upright,
arrested in midcheer,
her breasts defiant inside a lettersweater,
a triangle of her tights
exposed and magnetized,
more luminous, more precious than a goalpost.

Thus while the center and the guards,
the tackles and the ends plowed straight ahead,
the backfield scurried like lemmings to the shoreline,
to the open and upthrown form
of Tootsie Slocum.

For Toots never did screw
an interior lineman,
a discipline that added charm to charm:
though it also probably had a lot to do
with Galen Tucker's suicide,
not to mention Fairport's tragic
0-8 season.

SONNY

The boy had bad luck written all over his face,
According to Stocker:
Something about the tilt of the eyes,
The way they saw but never could quite focus.
Stocker said that sometimes people come that way
Straight from the shell,
Jostled too much by the hen, maybe,
Or the membrane scared loose by coyotes.
But in any such case the sign is there,
According to Stocker,
And clear as sin to the one with wits to read it.
So Sonny should have stayed in the egg,
Stocker said,
So poor in luck he'll bust his back one day
Picking shit with the chickens.

MAKING DO

The tops of all the sweatsocks
on the Cunningham High School gym
are disappearing,
are bunching downward
into damp discolored lumps
while the boys are practicing.

Who do not notice, or, noticing,
can not care.
Who have seen worse,
or have heard about it,
from a loved one or neighbor.
Elmira Bateman, for example,
a pin in her hip like a stovebolt,
whistles half the day
at gathering a dozen eggs.
Leroy Shannon waltzes the same tincan
all the way to the drugstore
with his mulberry leg.
Sadie Henderson has been half a century
at doctoring her bloody corns
with brown cotton hose
and a rayon smile.

It is not well to whine.
Thus the boys at practice
on the Cunningham High School gym
grin and leap on,
the tops of their sweatsocks
disappearing,
bunching downward
into the sweet malignant lumps
of precedent.

UNCLE DELMER

Chiefly there is the last discomfort:

We acknowledge it,
Bring in our tallest nurses,
Send jots of reassurance
To the kin.

Remember Uncle Delmer?
It was only a wart he had,
A friendly gathering of seed.
It killed him, of course,
But what we most remember
Is the way he cocked his head incredulously,
Like some encircled bird aware of children--
That, and the size our throats took
At his leaving.
Swollen,
They said the language like a crow
Grown used to capture,
Its feathers proud,
Its tongue healed hard as frets
Between the splitting.

MISS MAVIS CUNNINGHAM

A snapshot of Miss Mavis Cunningham,
rich little rich bitch's girl,
for weeks stayed stuck
to the door inside our outhouse.
Even the tiny snapshot
caught somehow the fire in Mavis' eye,
did passing justice to her saucy pride.
She had thick black hair,
dark as a banker's dreams,
and dimples that even from against the weathered door
called out for one's subservience.

Because Miss Mavis Cunningham,
rich little rich bitch's girl,
collected boys,
hoarded them like coins:
had more attendants than even Stud Halsey
could shake his famous dillywhacker at.
Which is why the Stud and I one late June afternoon
glued down the snapshot,
and locking ourselves inside before it,
day after summer day,
practiced our escape.

But we never quite made it.
Miss Mavis, her eyes relentless,
sat like an untouched goddess
at the center of our fantasies;
her charm, her money were simply too much
for our uncouth, unwashed little bodies.
So on the last day of vacation
we scraped the snapshot off the door,
and having grown both small and humble
floated its fragments into the dusk
of the outhouse hole.

THE EXQUISITE BEAUTY OF SOUTHEASTERN NEBRASKA

for Cliff Fawl

It is there like a postcard, he says,
And means it.
Space for grain and apples, right enough.
And for breathing.
Calls it something gaudy,
And don't care:
The exquisite beauty, say, of southeastern Nebraska.
Grins when he says it, too, like a gopher.
Speaks then of the smell of soil
Just last night rained on.
Is there gold in these here hills?
Ask the winesaps at Nebraska City.
The milo. The corncribs south of Bennett,
Dear as inlays.
(Did you know that kernels of hybrid seed
Are angels' eyeballs?)
Or question the shoreline of the Platte.
Do it however it pleases you,
But do it.
Touch it all, he says,
Even the lowdown price of hogs.
Let it run through your eyes
Like silt through fingers.
Then say something,
And mean it.
It is there like a postcard, for example,
This exquisite beauty of southeastern Nebraska.

Enough almost by god to make a fellow
Not ashamed to worship.

ANDY SILCOTT

Lived his life
like he played his pool,
according to Stocker:
couldn't shoot shape for shit.
So when the twilight years
bore down upon him,
Andrew F. Silcott found himself
jobless and penniless at the same instant,
his wife and his countless progeny
sifting their little brown hut to dust.
And wouldn't you know it,
one of them, sure enough,
uncovered a nugget:
a dead relation in Tacoma, Washington,
who had lived and expired looking only forward.
With the money
Andy bought a dumptruck,
became his own boss as a drayman.
Like playing slop-pool
against a perfect stranger,
Stocker said,
and at the showdown
shutting both eyes
and scoring.

COTTONWOOD

Teach us of roots,
Of the soft diurnal showering of seed.
Aware of soil and water, speak then to us of fire:
How driftwood moves on borrowed streams,
How elemental are the gatherings.
With branches splayed
Describe the broad blue seasons,
And their winds. Say it:
Because of me the roosted bird is tiny,
The lightning more than likely.
However then transected,
Chant with your breadth a liturgy of growth rings.
Ooze from your impacted pores
The simple juice of need:
Of roots, becoming as they are,
Of the soft diurnal showering of seed.

MR. R. K. BONHAM (RET.)

In his garden,
between the lettuce and the peas,
Mr. R. K. Bonham talks aloud
to the near end of a hoehandle:
he is setting straight again
that rare unfortunate day
of several years ago
when Fred the Chief Custodian
caught him napping in the boiler-room.
Like a puppet's head
the hoehandle nods,
seems to agree that Mr. R. K. Bonham
had been let loose prematurely.
Didn't Crazy Fred himself stretch out sometimes
beneath the bleachers,
or, what's worse,
sneak pliars and tapes and wrenches from the toolbox?
Now truthfully:
wasn't Fred the only reason
that Mabel Riley Ridgway
took to carrying a hogknife in her purse?
And who in this bloodthirsty Kansas world
is perfect anyway?
The hoehandle, smooth as a spoon,
keeps frantic answering:
yes and *yes* and *so they say* and *pshaw, Sir, nobody...*

VIRGINIA MAE GALLOWAY

Loved her so much
I tossed her lunchbucket
deep into D. S. Simpson's cowlot,
then hung around to watch the heavy-bellied Jersey
nibble at the spilled and curious contents.
Later, in the lunchroom, Virginia Mae Galloway
sat radiant in her suffering,
a cluster of disciples
asking what and who and why.
Virginia Mae, circumspect and stoic,
and more lovely than a rose,
nodded and answered guardedly.
Exactly what she told them
I should never know,
shall never care.
Only that precisely after school,
under the bridge near Marvel Roderick's greenhouse,
Virginia Mae Galloway was there.

HANGING AROUND

The comic books have been memorized,
and there is now no place but pockets
for inked thumbs. Free from chores,
the country boy, hanging around, chews his
tongue, studying pinballs. The bins
out home are filled with milo.
Jane has a cold. Saturday night
is slow with ice. Later, maybe,
when the pinballs lose their gloss,
a game of pool. Smoke. Powdered cues.
The casual click of chalk-pocked balls.
And tomorrow, after an early hard-on,
the unequalled stiffness of Sunday school.

VIRGIL

Rumor has it that Virgil
is somewhere yet in the area,
burning outbuildings.
At the age of 14 Virgil tossed a live punk
into the family hay.
At 15 he packed the family matchbox
and ran away.
Two weeks later,
a pallet of ashes and square-headed nails
smoldered the spot on Eldon Upshaw's yard
where a henhouse used to be.
After a year had passed, perhaps to the day,
Shorty Long stood sniffing the acrid tar
of what was left of his granary.
Then at intervals a woodshed,
a brooder, the rooted rafters of a leanto.
The squeals of protest
that shot from Alvin Crocker's hoghouse
carried south as far as Alva, Oklahoma.
Ellis Yoder's toilet blazed like a blue gem.
Virgil's daddy meanwhile
dug a raw ridge into his soft scalp, figuring.
Some say he went to hell like that,
still bloody, still wondering.
Others insist that though the old man died,
Virgil himself will never quite decay.
That for better or worse
he is the cool inflammable hero
of all of Barber County,
the rational cause
of all woe undeserved.

MRS. WILMA HUNT

Stocker said the air that came from
Mrs. Wilma Hunt
Had no more teeth in it
Than Prohibition.
He knew more than one woman just like that, he said,
Most of them sired no doubt
By dreams of cyclones.
Mrs. Wilma Hunt knew everything
There was to know
About nothing,
According to Stocker,
As if someone some time or other, he said,
Had twisted her one notch too tight,
Stripping the threads,
So that now she's like a cattle truck
On its way home,
The wind whistling Dixie
Through the slats of her sideboards,
The whole kit and caboodle
Going hellbent for election,
As Stocker put it,
But running empty.

MIDLANDS PROFILE: NOVEMBER

Around four o'clock the sun catches the country's best side.

    Beneath the hair of fresh stubble
    a podded land puffs
    high brown cheeks
    toward December.
    The flesh of soil is vast and cool,
    bulged,
    wound like a gift
    with wire whose barbs burst
    against a low sun's light.

Slatted grain bins go golden at the cracks.

A red deep-bedded truck sits near a barn,
half buckled under the unloaded pleasure of baled hay.

Two pheasants shuffle husks among the spilled
kernels of dinner.

Towns jut suddenly forward,
their elevators warm jowled with grain.

Wahoo. Swedeburg. Wisner. Scribner. Laurel,
all sending shards of shadow
to a late complected eastern landscape.

    The eye must count
    so fine a maze:
    each rich pock
    somehow photographed.
    Even the fallen seeds lie filled
    upon the portly face,
    genetic giants
    that wait like cattle to be fed.

And at the throat of scattered homes
the trunks of windbreakers: Pine. Cottonwood. Elm.
The switch of tamarack.
All a part of the profile,
all full lipped and facing north.

Fat, now, and quietly proud.

BUGGER RED BOWMAN

How in the Rexall Drugstore
after hours
Bugger Red Bowman
used to dry-dance
the pinball machine,
the waltz, the Saturday night stomp,
the two-step, the min-u-et,
something now fast, now slow,
improvised now, now conventional,
the oak legs of the machine
seeming to bend and sway,
joined as they seemed to be
to a warm firm malleable body,
its ornamental sides like thighs
following Bugger's perfectly fluid lead,
the two of them aglow with little lights
and the smart sassy chatter
of dingalings
as sweat described
the white diagonal scar
across Bugger's upper lip
and small delinquent boys
holding neglected comics
watched enthralled,
somehow knowing
that somehow something

in its own way
unspeakable

was taking place.

THE DYING OF MISS VALERIE TEAL

Miss Valerie Teal is dying tonight.
She is in her room, alone, repeating
Chaucer. Under soft Mazda lamplight
She works at strange words, memorizing
April. I see her sitting there,
Her clean bare feet tucked up and out
Of sight against the warmth of inside thighs.
She is intense, giving all her bursting fairness,
And all her eyes, to medieval rhythms.

It is a trip that she is taking
Alone, while I too sit alone
And listen to the April rain:
It strikes the mind
Like slim nails deftly driven,
Piercing the roots of droughted March
But dampening my own dark pilgrimage.

RHODES

Rhodes, the foreman, kept his uncluttered life
straighter than a T-bar.
An AT&SF timetable in a rear pocket
told him what to expect, and when.
He was almost never disappointed.
Except once, when a diesel slipped in
between the lines and caught him looking
the wrong way on his motor car. He freed
the drive belt and applied the brake.
But unlike the rest of us, he didn't
jump. He instead slapped at his pocket
for the timetable, and
seconds before the diesel nudged him
86.4 feet away into a ripe wheatfield
he managed a curious and begrudging glance
at the sweated schedule--
and next, looking up and at his crew,
just once he blinked.

Then in a perfectly logical sequence
he rose like a rag doll
off the hot (but parallel)
tracks of his Panhandle Division,
hoodwinked.

SOME DIRECTIONS FOR THE TOURING
OF SOUTHCENTRAL KANSAS

Drive west out of Medicine Lodge.
Breathe. The lungs go filled
With arrowheads. Weeds,
Clumped on mounded clay,

Whistle of painted ponies.
Listen. To the south are Kiowas,
Whooping history. Fences
Float like winded strands

Of hair, sun yellowed.
See. The pageant all is there,
The coppered flesh and the arrow
Straight as time, its flint tip

Red with new blue blood.
Know. You are galloping westward
Bareback over the shale
Of massacres, touring

Toward Dodge City, and
Treaties quaint as sunsets.

SAUNDERS COUNTY BARN

Try to ignore that Saunders County barn,
the one with the slatted, broken back,
where swallows in the dusk are homing.

Don't ask who the grandfather was
that called his milkcows to those brittle boards,
whether he had one offspring, or a dozen.

Don't concern yourself with the color of his teeth,
or inquire into the type of wood he fired
to burn the mortgage. Nor his wife:

whether she kept her wits past sixty,
or as a new bride drew blood when she
looked upon the back forty and bit her lip.

Nor their child, or children:
whether after one more final coat of paint
he/she/they hired an auctioneer. Or didn't,

and so hung on to be buried north of the toolshed.
Don't care whether the barn smells yet of dung,
whether the stanchions are yet slick

from the rubbings of cows' necks.
Don't bother even to ask after the swallows,
whether their droppings are mellowing in brittle hay.

Tell yourself that it has been a long and dusty day,
and that you must reach Wahoo by nightfall.
Thus, with firmness, tell the barn to go away.

Then glance at your rear-view mirror,
where, like a midget posing, relieving itself into the wind,
the barn grows smaller and smaller, then disappears.

Concentrate now on the road ahead.
Do not waste yourself on anything
lost, neglected, absent, weathered, or dead.

STOCKER

Said himself
he was planned laid out and constructed
on that green bench
in front of the pool hall,
that he had neither first name nor kin:
and no matter where you found him--
playing dominoes in the pool hall,
at breakfast in Bake's Cafe,
picking his teeth at the streetcurb,
whittling on the familiar green bench--
Stocker looked as if he had always been there
and had no intention ever of leaving.
For he was a huge man,
giant everywhere,
especially in the calves and belly,
looking a lot like a baby building.
Said as much himself,
and more than once,
each time grinning like a sophomore.
Even in his casket he seemed larger
than those of us looking on,
as if even in death
he had been given
the last word.

THE LOON AT NIGHT

1

At midnight the loon says it all:
Over cloud-shaded water the sudden sound
Abstracts the gaggle of day,
Startling even its echo.

2

Chest-deep in the cold lake water,
Moving deeper,
With sand fine as sugar underfoot,
I pause in the chill of the silence
That follows the last distant echo.
I am nude and refreshed to the chest,
With the cry of the loon in my ears:
I and the lake and the loon,
And the silence that follows all crying.

3

I walk deeper, then dive--and am scoured
By the cold lake water, and the thought
Of the loon floating somewhere,
Of the sound that has throttled the day.
I swim clean through the unrippled follicle
Of water and darkness. Daylight,
With its words, is behind me.
Tomorrow's declensions fall away.
There are only the lake and the loon,
And the silence that borne on the water says
Listen: this weird bird is best
When you have more than words to convey.

4

So sound off, loon.
With violence, on impulse, blurt nothing,
Maiming no one.
I am with you alone, swimming.
Tonight, at least,
Skinnydipping,
I stir at the heart of your world.

MEMENTO FOR REVENGE

Lest we neglect
to hate:
a severed ear,
a slit tongue,
an index finger
corded on a chain.

Remember the Alamo,
Pearl Harbor, and
elfin Hirohito
who with his legions
bambooed the fingernails
of Robert Taylor and John Wayne,

then decapitated
the local baseball star--
the one with blue Caucasian eyes
who as a child pitched papers
so daily on the hour:
Larry, or Jerry, what's-his-name.

SLEDDING WITH CHILDREN

I tell the children not to be afraid,
that in another life I served as mattress
to Her Majesty the Queen.
And they don't seem to disbelieve me,
laying small bundled bodies on my own,
forming pads so warmly welded
I sense the dissolving
of each bone and bootbuckle,
each tooth, each bitten nail,
all consumed in ice-bright air
atop the hill at old man Halstead's pond

until at some unmeasured point in time
we move,
the sled consumed now also,
its oaken slats
a layer of convivial skin
as we begin more rapidly to move,
sucking deep at the icy air,
our lungs joined in a sweet, mutual fear,
dry snow pelting the eyes as
we gain a tightening momentum,
our breath now lost like gauze unravelling,
impacted bodies slightly rocking,
slightly swaying,
until the speed is so great
we cannot see to be afraid,
the dry snow coming at the eyes
like instant slivers

and in a burst at last
we hit the snow-cleared pond,
let loose on ice so smooth
we ease our breathing--
while the sledrunners, warm with wax,
cannot desist,
and on and out we glide,
are gliding yet
touching carp and catfish,
tree and house and barn,
dismemberings now no more than shadows
spilled by winter's sun.

UNLONELINESS POEM

for my wife, after 20 years

Let us shake hands.
Rub noses.
Press unshod feet.
Skin of skin,
we seek
the impervious covering
to wrap our isolations in.

And though it is
as always
only tissue,
brief as morning,
we go at least that
single span unlonely
in the joining.

AUNT DORA

This isn't so bad, she said, meaning the migraine.
Then to her most explosive varicose: I have seen much worse than this.
At Uncle Fred's incredulous rites she stole the audience.
More gruesome things have happened, she said, and to better men.

She had a hair wart on her chin,
And when I touched it at a family gathering
She said it's nature's way of varying beauty.
Her cancer, working slowly, gave her time to shrink,
Her frame at last so insignificant it muffled visitors.
So always she spoke for them: slow, owlish words
That shook the medication on the nightstand.
This isn't so bad, she said, meaning the loss of flesh.
Then to the space above her flatted breasts:
I have seen much worse than this.

And thus she disappeared,
Her last breath sucking deep to start again
That certain fiction.

JOGGING

Moving to make the world move
I jog on heavy legs
Over the soft pine needles of ages,
Over the compression of brown leaves,
Following a distended line of lime
Left from late Spring by young
Cross-country boys who ran

For medals and for glory--
By lithe long legs that spun
Aspen and ash peripherially
Into the past,
That reached with certain cleated feet
Into the future,
Borne by sinew too timeless

For trivial time--by legs
Impossibly not mine,
That now,
Jogging,
Stretch chiefly up and down,
Moving begrudgingly to make
A begrudging earth move,

Following the pale lime line
Under the Spring boys'
Ash and aspen, while
Sensing the slow rush of August air
Against a vision
Of late-summer lichen,
Of panicles and powdered leaves,

Of woody sumac,
Of the milky juice of
Reborn petal clusters, while
Knowing in tightened bones the
Symbiotic jolt of each step's contact,
The jumping of heavy flesh as,
Jogging,

I follow the convenient line
Out of one man's public forest
Into the unleafed bewilderment of
Another, but always and forever
Jogging,
Seeing a new lime line where
No boy during

No late Spring
Ever ran, the chimerical line
A guiding scar on the huge
And night-time face of anarchy--
Before and under the
Softskinned feet of only me,
Jogging.